B O N E F L U T E

Poems For All Seasons

Ruth F. Harrison

Illustrations by Marilyn McLaughlin

CAPE PERPETUA PRESS

First printing
ISBN 1-888934-15-8
Library of Congress Catalog Card Number 96-84664

Some of these poems were first printed in the following publications:
*West Wind Review; Denver Quarterly; Interstate; The International
Journal of Communicative Psychoanalysis and Psychotherapy; Calapooya
Collage;* and *Montage.* Some have appeared, as Oregon State Poetry
Association contest winners, in *OSPA Newsletter.*

Contents

A flute, made of a dead man's bone,
                           makes all things drunk;
the wine-bowl of the holy night
                           spilled at the brim ...

                    --Nikos Kazantzakis, *Odyssey*

I owe more thanks than I can say to my beloved family and friends,
especially to Fred Harrison, to Shirley DeVoss, to my writers'
group, and to Clyde A. Beakley, poet, whose unstinting support
helps make this edition possible. Hey thanks, gang-- thanks for the
moments, for the faith, and most of all for the joy in wordwork.

                                        Ruth F. Harrison
                                        Waldport   '96

on keeping

set it free, let it go
let the wind take it;
to have's not to know--
set it free, let it go.

though it shakes me to know:
to keep is to break it--
set it free. let it go--
let the wind take it.

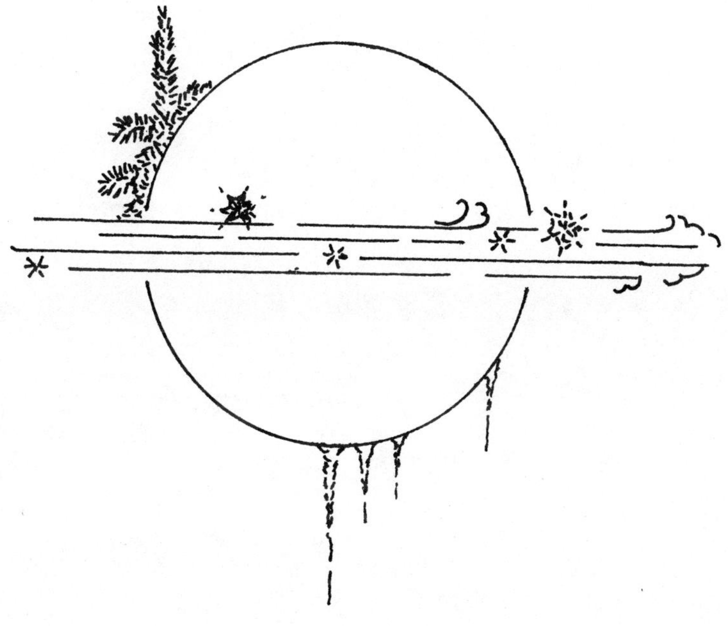

Part 1

Winter

Night

North

bottom of the canyon

riverbed

snowdrift

freeze

water

icicles

skis

wind

glacier

North Star

bare branch

frozen ruts

blue shadows

snowflake

last song

we listen, now, to the last song:
after the gold, the cold
after the glow the bare stripped bone
the purpling tundra

silver trail behind me, twin lines entwined
link me to houses, a house, one warm room
fireside, voices, soft laughter, the sound
of wooden spoon stirring in a metal pot,
frost patterns on window glass, steam-- "my
  people weave it this way for warmth and
  for good fortune" "Try it-- it is
  made from the milk of reindeer" --too

late. I have whistled aurora to the ground
woven light with my fingers-- play
play with me O and heaven's fire is cold
and the last chimneysmoke is vanished
in skydark-- gone beyond gone. --I carry
this so-cold heart burning blue, a lantern
for the black tortoise
to see beyond hope.

In the ninth circle the ice is deep:
last song of the west is north.

winter lantern

legs

long blue

shadows on

flamelit crunching

snow

Useful Expressions in Sweden

what is this
what is the charge
do you speak

I don't understand
please speak more slowly
when does (anything) arrive
please repeat

where can I find
in which direction is
please direct me to
please point

where is my baggage is it
near
far
very far north
south
east
west
is the road

I would like a room with single bed, with two beds, with
bath, without meals--
please, the key

I want this pressed, cleaned, washed, repaired, I
want it rare
when will anything be returned: women
men working
it's hot it's cold, it's raining, it's snowing, what fine
weather
dangerous, go slow, exit ...*please point*.

place

where form and chaos meet
          lies a (boundless) boundary
beyond which That
          where breakers turn and buckle ...
          deeps swirl, furl ...
                sands mesh and hush, pebbles'
                      susurrus ...

here
    skin is irrelevant
          even enclothed, enhoused--

seawater sings in the heart
    tide beats in the pulse
          kelp catches in the cranium
                gull nests on the skull

the Seven Seals open round eyes
    on the shore watcher
          ever new form-stuff
                bubbles up singing
    revelations not closed in
                leather bindings

Sufi Tale: Where It Went[1]

What grace we tap that we may say I SAW:
Mostly we surmise, and like A CHILD
CARRYING A LIGHT, edge forward, feet
quicker than our head would be, fearing some
    primordial grab from the dark around us.
Yet if I ASKED
    WHERE DID THE LIGHT COME FROM?
drawing on daily answers: battery, match,
    star, moon, wall-switch, sun--
we've light enough to make all plain
    clear, featureless, sans mysterium

    (until the dark-night moment when we
        wonder-- should
        HE PUT IT OUT, how then--?
and say ... how then? and should he say--?
What would we answer if HE SAID
    TELL ME, if you have understanding,
        WHERE IT IS GONE ...?

)

<hr>

[1]The tale told in capital letters is attributed to Hasan
of Basra; from Idries Shah, *The Way of the Sufi*, p. 227.

After

(for Mer-lyn, January 1990)

Silence of storm, after the four-day blow:
We pick up our flat selves and open wind-shut eyes
on broken glass and trees, and broken child.

Nobody asked the question to this answer
more final than night, less plausible than forever:
For ocean's daughter the tide sings a sand song
and the quick river hushes.

in the heart of the burning giant

on a day
when unknown blissed-out black poet floor-sits
between MEN doors opposite my office
sketching out poems while formal I confer
with polite student
"ruth and john--john and ruth--sitting in bliss"
makes ecstatic staticky phonecalls to publisher
in los angeles, on a day
when angel announces "your face knows
some marvelous secret" on a day
when arm crooked round my neck from behind is
kin-warm and little and cheek
grazes my hair O lose me not
on a day

or it could be a leaf whirls three times round and
steps down stairs of air
or venus westering low in clearnight blue
or this creek curling round dimpled water
or now wrong number answers my ring "Rain Company:--"
then feet of grass make speed enough
freeway to work a path of light

then naming alone suffices, *be* becomes
active verb
and life a gift-horse whose teeth
pass inspection

No It Is Opposition

pausing on black and surf-washed stone
  a shape, almost invisible in sea-wrack,
the arctic tern is but
  a visitor on our shore, shoal-seeking
it is in transit, always in transit
its one-way trip eleven thousand miles
                              its arctic turn
its eleven-thousand mile journey
                        its antarctic pause
its eleven thousand miles
                        the arctic tern has
distance, its gaze sees distance ...

how can a worded species tell its miles?

each wing-beat is pure tern, no surplus
stripped to the simplicity of its aim
its cry the loss of any warm fixed thing

its hatching, its nest-time to one end,
this winging, this taught endurance
that has learned to will one thing

the arctic tern, almost invisible, a hope, a form
pausing on black stone at ocean-edge

Noitisoppo Si Ti On

... promise her anything, but ...

When I believe your promises again,
your steadfast hands that, generous and sure,
guided me where you liked; and yes, that pure
idealist look that has the strength of ten--

When I believe your speaking eyes, and when
mindless I follow on your guided tour,
when I will brave your weather and endure
what storms may please you, trust the words you pen--

Then rolls Columbia backward to her source;
then sands are numbered, and then Argus sleeps;
Hell turns one block of ice; the vasty deeps
are desert; then rejoicing is remorse.
When yesterday's tomorrow, then sir, then
will I believe your promises again.

The Eve of the Year: A Madrigal in Frozen Form

12

Thin powder-dry snow drifts wraithlike in windrows
pattering out on housewalls like fineblown sand
mellow in lamplight; blue, blue in cool shadows.

Walkways are frozen silent and crossed and fanned
with white-quiet drift of cold stuff dropped midflight:
Water no longer water. It wasn't planned--

Nobody needed this weather. Roads at night
crisscrossed by snowghosts, shimmer silver with ice;
weighted cypresses shiver and droop in white.

Crystalline sky holds thin-carved moon: precise
too small for light-- some jeweler's fair device.

One hour to go. Thirteen degrees to zero.
Hole up. Stay warm. Drink deep. Watch for tomorrow.

dream before spring

… wandering in a far dry place without guide.

You were too sleepy, Soul,
to come along, I have no blame for you.
It only means-- going alone.
The way lies nerveless, indifferent; all perspectives
same enough: dry, bare,
no one direction marked with colored stones.

… a desert place: no growing bush
nor cactus flower nor blade of grass
interrupts its settled sands.

Sometimes I weep in it, but tears
too salt to water life--. The ground
is sowed with salt.

Laugh in it, sometimes, but don't much like
the arid sound, since jackals take it up
nor wince to hear the thing they make of laughter.

Sometimes I talk in it, craving
some sound
this silent way. Lacking one bird,
could there be chanting?

Sometimes I think to make
of silence my companion, bread-sharer. But voices
in the skull conspire to cheat away that solace,
discoursing on desert places,
empty lands, a sand-lodged cranium,
or dreaming a half-remembered flowering tree …

Dream, then …? Was a fair place, once
as in a courtyard near the sea
swept with bright air,
walkways broidered with spice-borne flowers
pinks and sweet williams …

a summerhouse, eight-sided:
arches looking out ... butterflies
floated about among the columns
... a walled garden.
At center, a fountain--
a fountain, a tree
a fair and flowering tree.
Wishing tree, was it?
People were drawn to
lay a hand on the wood of it
touch it wish it well, and wish
for themselves something perhaps inchoate
the tree made them remember.

Drifts of white bloom, dark branches
... petals dropped on stone rimming the fountain
or marked the ripples widening, the pool ...

                    --Promises.

Sky stretches vast, here in the flatlands, blue and
                              waiting.

Hawk waits, yet I hold no fear of him.

... Time, though, 's a vulture
distant enough and black, and yet identified
by the plane of his soaring:
                              sure.
His eye is sure.
He has his eye on me.

I do not fear him, either, yet I
know (oh, for the rod of Moses--)
                    he'll kindly clean my
              bones, leaving white arches a
              summerhouse for ants--

and a column of felled vertebrae
              where nothing flowers.

Be

... but the one word: be ...

Sliding down crystal planes come single words
to build a frame (not cage) to house the spirit
for those who "spiritless against economy"
stay.

(Set in this frame: a howl of wind, a charcoal

<table>
<tr><td>

ivory black
now sky
hail
lightning
--white breaker
far out.
Close in, a
white-green
seethe, a curl
of phthalo green
Under it all
the question:
</td><td>

be.
</td><td>

sweep
of sea
sea-grass
flattened in a
low, seeking
gale
lone gull
making no
headway
tilt and
swerve--
fanfold--
</td></tr>
</table>

how to hang a dome of light above
deep pression, cession, cessation, and recession
where thieves leave thank-you notes and poor give waybread
to farers crying over the stone-dark sea.

Part 2

Spring

Morning

East

crocus

climbing path

arbutus

open

air

swing

spring water

compost

water lily

trillium

lilac

sunny glade

wild strawberries

creek

in the beginning Was

but this white insistence is too much
Words dry in my brain.
your probable eyes render them insufficient
and How shall i create reality with them?
and How shall i begin?

Yet I remember a day Jud made with a word
lilies and banks of snapdragon kneehigh
waist-high along the walls of my windowless office
Quince bloomed in the hall

and this morning
frederick-the-magnificent
glittering by on his moon-plated diamond-wheeled
                              unicycle
scattering yellow roses O

O the glance notice the spent second of glory-giving how
            sudden as a word and singing the day turns
                        colored

Home-Place in April

here, beside the old house
here where lilacs arch roof-high shade
her purple journey breathes home scent
shadows fill her arms
bouquets of deep lost summers
and not a fragrant step
but holds, golden, dust of days gone
of the long passing

arranged in a vase
by a blondish girl with thin arms.
Choosing the Stella vase
she guides the stems to stand tall
dizzy with color
deep-drawn scent; the line and softness
suffuse indoors, outdoors, make old
footprints spill with purple

For My Sister in Her Work and Time

She sits over a green silk slipper-case,
the gentle curve of her shoulder inviolate over time.

A window arcs light across her face, her lap
where work lies idle. How bright the needle
between stopped, sure fingers. Loop of thread
catches the sun, lingers. She stitches, turns the
        green cloth. Stops. Will stitch again.

It was a cold castle, all this long winter.
She could sketch in frost with her finger
on any stone slab of it, inside, in the stair,
                anywhere--
except for mantlepieces, it was all rimed in white
and her breath fanned out in crystals. Now, though,

Sun touches the hills, silken in coming green
and every wooded ride waits to blossom,
      shapes buds,
        will sing,

The air waits, breath stops with it, something
               is

        coming

Comes with the sun, and she holds green pleasure,
softly turning the unmeasured work
in fingers not too stiff for thread and needle
and waiting for the tread upon the stair
of him who with the coming spring is
      surely
        almost there.

Spring Final

In your brown hair and yellow dress, you stay
Longest of all on this last day of spring
And write, and pause, and write, and twist your ring
Your face alive and quiet, your costume fey
Enough to draw you out to join the day
That waits across the threshold, blossoming.
Your hair a curtain, you work lingering
Over this final choosing what to say:
As though this were your favorite thing to do,
You grace the hour. I'd swear you have not seen
Him waiting, shy, hoping to speak to you--
The backrow, quiet young man, whose eyes are green,
Whose face betrays his hope, joy, pain, duress
Caught in your brown hair and your yellow dress.

WR 121: Impromptu Day

The squeaking persists. Yet I have said my words
maybe for always. Certainly for this hour.
The pens should move in breathing stillness. Now
unease sits on shoulder angles, ankles, hands--
and chairs dance crooked in the greenish light
we spend our daylife in. Help for it, is there--? or
have we now come too far down a wrong way
for anything to better? The walls are indifferent:
the faces bloom. The light is bad.
There is no window. It is spring-- we know it
partly by the distance grime extends
around the ceiling vents: almost a year's worth.

Daphne bloomed-- daphne-- years ago this morning
against the wall. We will find sunshine later
if life lasts. --It's better now--
pens move, paper silences mean the hush
hushed peace, peaceful stillness, still anguish,
anguished effort of the work of words proceeds.
... We should have died hereafter ... there
would have been a time, but to have died
heretofore seems unjust immurement. Well, Montressor--
you've built our tomb of books; the word endures
past flesh and bone, past stone and concrete. So
there will be no undoing. In the beginning
was-- and will be.

When We Were Very in Time

(a dialogue with A.A. Milne
with love to Christopher Robin)

I can remember
>   WHEN I WAS ONE
>   being old and wise:
>   I HAD JUST BEGUN.

I got my first toothbrush
>   WHEN I WAS TWO
>   and on that birthday
>   I WAS NEARLY NEW.

I spilled green ink
>   WHEN I WAS THREE
>   on my pink dress--
>   I WAS HARDLY ME.

I could button my pjs
>   WHEN I WAS FOUR ...
>   about three feet tall ...

>   I WAS NOT MUCH MORE.

I gathered wild bluebells
>   WHEN I WAS FIVE
>   and inside the house
>   I WAS JUST ALIVE.

>   BUT NOW I'M SIX
>   ...   plus fifty-one

>   I'M AS CLEVER AS CLEVER
>   till clever is done;

>   SO I THINK I'LL BE SIX NOW
>   plus fifty-two ...

>   FOREVER AND EVER
>   till ever is new.

Luve Hath Manye Thinges

(Welsh form: *cyrch a chuta*)

Luve hath time but no countree,
Luve hath person, she and hee.
Luve's discryminating eye
Chuses, keeps, doth sense defye.
Luve hath charme, will not lette be;
Luve hath endynge, as we see.

'Luves me' turns to 'luves me not'
In a thoght, when luve's not free.

Word

Spirit breathes on the sea:
So comes creation--
Speaking the one word: be
Spirit breathes on the sea.

Speaks stegosaur, Iceland, knee,
Speaks granite, frostbite, nation ...
Spirit breathes on the sea--
So comes creation.

two cinquains

1

Nothing
but the beat, beat
of my quiet heart can
compete with surfsounds on this full
moon night.

2

Child, I
remember you
in blue bunny slippers:
How do you come to me wearing
gray hairs?

place of arches

beyond the arches of the mind
is such a place as was never

o as was never ...

here iswas and evershallbe slide by
side
nowthen dances near and far ...

Blessed be good, the fabric
of this our tastefully designed
oh patchwork
Blessed the name beyond speaking
and the voice that names us good.
Blessed the spring of being,
freshet and blade
Blessed the joy that answers the
holy nudge--

Good is the earth, ground of
our being
Good the air, loving us,
medium of messages.
Good is the living water--fish
ride it, leaves
hide it, it is
clear, it is--
Good the fire-- dross-burner
sign
source
light
to see how dances iswas and nowthen, near
and far,
see evershallbe ripple, spindrift thin
among four posters of
the archéd mind ...

Treble Clef: Tanka

29

songbirds on five wires
against gray unfeatured sky
fluff yellow feathers
sing spring *a cappella* notes
on a score in common time

texas as a state of mind

'Beautiful, beautiful ...' Grandma used to sing
sitting, wheelchair, living-room corner,
eyes lifted to white windowlight, yarns and needles
forgotten in her lap, she seeing beyond walls
beyond house and Colorado's ring mountains
to fields of blue, bluebonnets
sparked with Indian Paintbrush or
just plain. Acres, perfumed hills of blue
Lupinus texensis ... 'kinda like'
my mother said, 'the lupine you pick when you
go gathering flowers.' But different Grandma said--
nothing
could compare with Texas bluebonnets, blue hills
a-folding on and on to forever. Myself,
I thought Texas must be God's place, or at least
where better could God think to go and play,
wade fragrant blue, see
land's hills and gullies blue blanketed,
go running, and fall down, and run again,
buoyant in blue.

About the Pupil

--for the circle of light-benders, WR 242
January 1990

Dilate, resolve, contract ... what is this eye
       opening, closing in our classic place?
Seers from birth, we ring an empty space
       and looking in, look outward ... roof... sky--
Hesitant, like iris petals-- shy
       yet radiant of ourselves, we seek out ways
to catch light, image, essence in a phrase
       transposing truth to feed the inner aye.

An iris opens on a world inverse:
       inverted things turn upright past the lens.
These poets' eyes, shaping chaos as verse,
       link earth and spirit, opposites, as friends.
  And each dilation in our classic hour
focuses light for some fine center power.

Time Lapse

I wish someone had thought to set up the cherished
  box camera, snap the picture of them helping
  one another with their hair:

waist-long, heavy, honey-hair and dark,
  the two heads near each other,
    light catching the curve of arms, the
    hands dividing, braiding

the braider standing (my later mother, I think:
  younger sister); older sister
    sitting, impatient it be

done. Both ready, eager to be off, to bundle
  their good dresses rolled behind the
    saddle, ride eleven miles to the

box supper at the schoolhouse, carrying decorated
  offerings: supper boxes, cake-cover hiding
    Royal Tropicaroma cake ...

Catch them at that getting-ready moment: window-light
  from behind, shining on hair (a decade later bobbed
    tucked into a miniature cedar chest, coils
    today still bright as

the day of the shear decision, though Stella (dark,
  rosy) died a new mother in 'Thirty-three, while
    Mary (quick, bright-haired, skinny) died
    silvered-over in May of 'Eighty-five);

catch the readying moment, their calf-length gingham
  dresses, window-light on their hair, fingers
    deftly braiding, faces a little
    shadowed, forever

young. Edge of the iron stove behind them, off
  focus. Hand-embroidered curtain at the window-
    side, wooden chair-back turned aslant out of

the way, long fall of hair, the modest sleeve and bodice
        of the dress, soft impatient drape of the sitter's
            skirt, Sears shoes (called Maryjanes

buttoned strap across the instep), hairbrush laid aside
        on the wooden table ....

Save in the photo this ordinary moment ... sisters.
        The task is daily-- daily the hair must be brushed
        and brushed and brushed, combed

till the deep tangles smooth, brushed silken, parted,
        braided
                tied with a bit of ribbon hemmed from a scrap
                        of the gingham cut for the dress

before they set the yeast to rise and fire up the stove
        to heat the water for the hundred thirty-four
                pieces of wash to be washed on the washboard
                        to be wrung by hand, and swished in

the first rinse tub, and wrung by hand, and swished
        in the bluing rinse and wrung by hand, and hung
                with clothespins on the line, one by one
                        by hand, and

fix noon dinner for the threshing crew-- kneading dough,
        harvesting carrots, potatoes, from the adobe soil
                catching and killing a young rooster,
                        scalding, plucking, dressing out

cutting up, frying, setting the rolls to bake, chopping
        apples, walnuts, cabbage; mashing, buttering
                making gravy

serving: iced tea, lemonade, gallons ... and dishes, the
        whole twelve-serving set, washed in drawn
                well-water with bar soap, scalded

from the steaming teakettle, dried with floursack
        towels (embroidered), and shelved clean in the
                pantry till

suppertime. Bringing in line-dried clothes, folding,
        mending, darning, dampening ready for the three
            sizes of the flatiron. Laying out a
                    pattern--

dress, shirt, apron, or working out a new design or
        piecing on the Dresden Plate quilt, or catching
            up-- hoeing, weeding-- in the gardens,
                    feeding the new-hatched chicks

gathering sawed wood and scraps of kindling to fill the
        woodbox, tonight's and tomorrow morning's fires.
            It would be nice had

someone caught them so
                    for all time
                            the waist-long hair rippling
        unbraided, the brushing, combing, parting
            shining, glowing, getting
                    ready for a party.

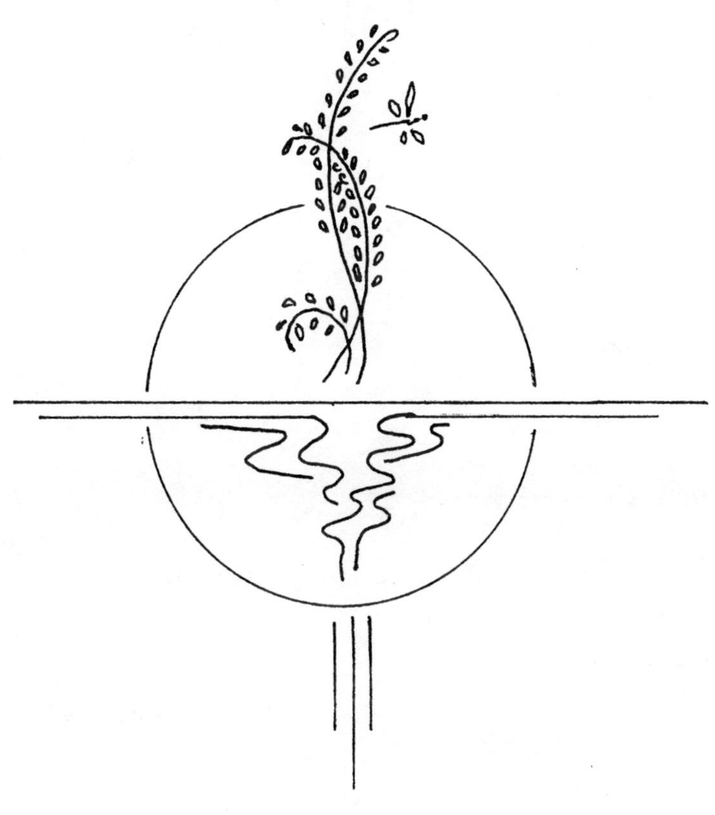

Part 3

Summer

Midday

South

hilltop

mesa

lupine

blaze

earth

hoe

tall corn

squash

field

Indian Paintbrush

silver maple

willow

river

dust

Secret

37

Keep it under your hat--
It will thrive in the warm sun-speckled dark
the magic cave of criss-crossed black heavens
          and slow-moving stars
               and tickly summer grass.

     Seasons wheel
          summer on summer, gold
               in an afternoon-- I know
I spent my straw-haired girltime there.

Sometime Song

If I should cross the pasture of your mind
edging along the creek and through the fence
and not be set upon nor driven thence
and gather what there flowering I find--

If you'd permit the trespass, yet not bind
the trespasser, nor take it as offense
that I've purloined some sunlight, colors, scents--
green shadow-thoughts with memory entwined,

Let nothing in you falter at my daring,
steady your heart like patient meadowland,
sweet be your course, old friend, and eased of caring,
light be my footprint where in your grass I stand.
Glad beyond speech I am once more to see
you with your silent blessing love me free.

before beginning

... but words desert.
Before me reach sand distances
--lines of surf surge to me
        to me, relentless

yet (from this half-mile's
                high angle) gentle
                    ageless

a blue gray green, soft
                steel
    streaked with violet.

Wind swerves in to
    stir my staring hair.

Beyond this next stone
        balustrade, grasses
dip and lean, querying a
                clover
conversing with spring
                cones,
    long-leaf pine.

It's not that they fail me, words
            those oldest mainstay--
it's that (given these blind-sighted
            distances, given
        what gulls do in planes of light, given
            the slow grass gestures, the slope's
            light raiment)

        words cannot rise ...

Sestina Lente

Love should be in it, for counting life counts love;
add: one golden chaintree, as twig leads to blossom,
          as rivulet to river.
Knowing must be in it, that born is to be lost--
          loss not of our making
but intertwined with reasons why a clock.

We have been true to rendezvous with clocks
since sages tell us time is scant for love
          and less for making--
that what's in bud today tomorrow is past blossom
          the fallen petal lost
yellow reflection floated down, down river.

In my green time the ways were all one river:
only long forever parents knew the clock …
          lost, lost …
What fastens once-upon-a-Wednesday to today is love
          and this day's blossom
is a good given, not of our making.

I've seen her mirrored and no: she is not what I was making--
I was making her juniper desert flint river
          mossflower, indian paintbrush blossom
bluebell larkspur blackeyed-susan four o'clock …
          Sagebrush. Foxglove …
but gathered once is all; and the pathways are lost.

Death drops abysses: each brink to the other is lost--
can you remember, last time, what that was you were making--?
          Whom did you love?
Did her spirit lave you cool and forever a river?
Had you finished when the clock
stopped? when frost blacked and shriveled the blossom?

Say time is yet for a twig? one bud, one blossom--?
an apple before the good season is lost …?
          Ah, the cold clock
decrees hand and soul have no further kinship with making …
          Soon, soon we will thrust on the river:
Then lost-- clocktime and blossom and making and love.

Blossoms will no longer be in the world of our making--
lost, wide and wider, swept far and swift on the river:
clocks foraged yesterday, early, on white-blooming love.

Near the River of Thy Delights

Watch:
        the Hour arrives that
          no woman knows ... yet
              nor no man

Wake:
        for sun has startled shadows
          splendor falls
            on tower walls, opens flowers

Moveless
        let it pass
          like summer boys running
              over long grass

Sleepless
        dark watcher, cobrawise
          looks hooded forth, uses
              your eyes ...

Behold
        a nothing, a purple, a conversation
          with a parking meter,
            three goosegirls laughing
              man in tartan and patches
                and old yellow golf sox
        color swirls, green, a purple
          a nothing

Wait
        a nothing

Stay ...
        the bridegroom yet arrives

Bone Flute, Drum of Human Hide

Sing. Sing. And if you be consumed in fire
hints of a morning light outshine the burning:
what tempers swords makes music in the lyre.

Keen is the note struck from tight-twisted wire,
the tone brought true by tension on tension turning--
Sing. Sing so, if you be consumed in fire.

We try our steel in water, blood, desire;
something the Saracens knew we keep relearning:
what tempers swords gives music to the lyre.

Cradled in embers, ah see the golden flyer,
proud bird on fire-shod feet, who, ashes spurning,
sings. Sing so, if you be consumed in fire.

Dead bones sing for the dancer's steps; the pyre
transforms the flesh to song for those sojourning:
what tempers swords makes music in a lyre.

Shatter the dying coals, and the sparks fly higher:
seeds they are, life, outreaching the dead flames'
                              yearning.
Sing. Sing. So if you be consumed in fire
what tempers swords gives music to your lyre.

Song: 'I Am That'

Shall I compare ... Thee ... to a summer's day?
"Thou art more temperate..." sustaining all
the dance of atoms: butterflies, the small
pulse of the blood, the redwood tree, the hay.

Tigers walk at thy will, and puppies play.
Movement is in thy hands: prowl, flight, and
                                        crawl
dance in thy dance, and need no protocol.
Thou art the light, the spirit, and the way.

Oh, light that feels-- oh day that knows no night
loving, creating, granting-- giving zest
webbing the spaces of the universe,

we move not, but Thou movest us-- the rest
is but illusion and will soon disperse:
Thou art the dance, the webwork, and the light.

place of breath

this birthday universe, pipe of soaply chaos, Breathed through
makes parti-colored shapes, so to create
huckleberry, gopher, jimson weed, chipmunk,
alder
dandelion, black rose, billy goat--
billy club--
Billy Eckstein, Billy Daniels, Billie Holiday
Holiday
holiday ...
the bubbles rise, and are
and are
unique
and are
no more--
so much for bubbles, things
of skin and shining
inarguably there/not-there.

Breath--?
--It may be breath of god, wind of god, spirit of god
gathers itself four-footed
plumy-tailed
walks with me, over me, before me, to the bluff
unworded friend, rabbit-sniffing shadow--

--It may be new bubbles rise, forgotten songs
form and breath, form and breath
(breath breathed in, breathes out
[some times])
--it may be the festival is alive, though
there is no new holiday this
gloomy sun day ...

Three Thirty-Three

45

Bright on the bluff, hawks wheel and stoop;
low in the meadow, cattle call;
shadows lie long, and rushes droop.

Edge of the meadow, alders tall;
house on the hill, sweep of heather--
road rounds over the river. Small

bridge in the east; storm-clouds gather
high in the light and dark of sky,
landscape livid in yellow weather ...

Stump in the meadow, crows nearby
scatter and scold and lift and swoop
black on the ground, but wings on high ...

Between Time

It is the magic hour:
    shadows on earth lie long.
The primrose folds its flower ...
    it is the magic hour.

Twilight comes filled with power:
    silence-- a single song ...
It is the magic hour--
    shadows on earth lie long.

Empty Form

(for BJG, 1925-1992)

you   homeplace of death is ours   let
in my   shadowland, old desert whence   me then
heart's blue chamber   no farer returns.   be clear, while
wrapped silent in amber   Of living   death is avatar: "Yet
tell me, why do you   what   a few days, and thou
lie here so somber?   remains? only   the evercircling sun
In your closing   some word spoken   shall see no more."
I die   some   deed   acted,   and   Till when,
too   some thing handmade, unbroken-- see

Rivertime

Remembering the summer river, how
     shadowed its waters, the
       deep song of its current,
old cottonwood dipping a branch, willows
         low-hanging over sandbar,
horseflies,
     mosquitoes, yes …
 slant of late sun,
      silver reflections, eddies dimpling,
whirlpools, round tumbled river-rock,
     how as children we lingered on shady banks, in
       shallow backwaters, how a dragonfly sparked sudden
       red blue bronze under
tamarisk blossoms over green waters, how
russian olive silver-lined the road, how
     sagebrush edged Uncle Clyde's south pasture--
time folds. The river is here.

Feel it now: hot dusty sunlight;
cold meniscus our feet break
     through, ankles take the chill, calves …
     Our feet arch on moss-slippery rocks, we go deeper--

     plunge neck-deep into measureless cold.

                 Ah!

Mudcrawl. Paddle out … we feel the channel
     its dark tug-- scare each other with
      tales of power,
     our strength small as
      our bodies in that
     heavy green seeking ….

Last hour of sunlight:
     We build a log raft.

Rivertime: summer's best gift.
  cool grace for our hot working day;
both reward and warning confirming our childhood;
          solace for hay-chaff's itch, promising dangerous
futures and the beauty and majesty of
                    cool Japanese museums:
willows' green grace, slow swirling eddies
          gray water-skippers consulting reflections--
          sky underfoot, and pink tamarisk bloom
                water-cooled sunlight
          brothers in cut-off overalls, Daddy
      in his old one-piece black bathing suit
        and Mama in her non-swimming green ...
          tow-heads, little sisters--

Being long in years and of
          sound mind, I do devise and
                give and bequeath to
          heritors here (let this
                one wish
              be so)... each child its
                personal river
with dragonflies, quicksands, sparkle
                              and fear.

      Think river, and summer
            is:

        the waters all power, sun and
          shadow, clean bitter scent of cottonwoods

                    the afternoon hour ...
          leaves starting to turn ...

Part 4

Autumn

Sunset ... Twilight

West

balanced rock

canyon wall

aspen leaf

flare

fire

basket

granary

woodpile

hillside

purple asters

woodbine

hazel wood

ebb tide

mist

A Plain Song Then

Don't sing her dirges.

She goes
      as always
           clutching a book, a sketchpad
               crying wait for me--

see, she's bouncing on the front-seat edge
                 watching the road unfold
         tasting the next
           traveling light
           and lightly.

          Don't sing her dirges.

Skip the incense ...
           change, always, was spice enough.

    Flowers? --She loved them growing. Dandelions
                         especially ...

You might pick her some dandelions, although
      I think the sight would make me cry for
                  knowing
          she loved them growing.

Round Seasoning

seed
dry, brown
soaking, swelling, cracking
soften, burst, yield, sprout
emerging, greening, uncurling
lush leafed
squash

bloom
half open
widening, lifting, petaling
orange, bright, big, sunny
wilting, tattering, drying
tassel end
butternut

butternut
green, pale
whitening, plumping, tanning
suave, curved, silken, gold
burgeoning, rounding, browning
picked, cooked
ambrosia

table
mother, father
gathering, enfolding, holding
girl, grandmother, boy
sitting, encircling, quieting
bless, break
supper

the turning year

This is a turning year.
My mother moves in an old country
where no thing is matter
and on this land lies
change beyond speaking.

The cottonwoods know her passing--
they've mourned my father these
six years past.
Earth of 'this little farm'
lifts to no answering footfall.
Lawn chairs hold
air
a curled leaf;
the house all elbows,
shaping itself to edge presences
defines itself, like clay, by
a hollow at the center.

Of white hens now there will be
no new generation,
great brown eggs gathered warm
--no more--
yet I remember how in spring
she carried the yellow chick
in her apron pocket
--like a schoolgirl, small and shy--
loving littleness and warmth.
"Careful, Mama. He's just a baby."

Her gnarly thumb tested chick-down
all of her holding him, except
her memory
(holding facts now as water
holds oil)

"Let me take him now--?"
                              "... what?" vaguely.
"I'll put the little fellow with the others--?"
"... oh. All right ..." But her hands
having their own minds, house this
                  small warm
a moment yet before they too
                  forget.

When she was twenty-eight and I was three,
                  her secret hands
(her eyes smiling, face bright with
                  edge-of-winter cold)
brought some small peeping
close beside my cheek ...
                  --ah, warm
                                    ah, soft--
a perfect understanding held us three
                  in one warm center
mother, child, and chick:
"This is how a new thing is that never was,
living, on this earth before ..."
a life, where was just space
and nothing, before ...

The final hens walk
                  curious on this clay
                  feathers askew
          foot raised, forgotten--
eyes searching earth
                  for something without word ...
Cell by cell 'this little farm' empties its life
                  buildings lose definition
                  fieldmice encroach
                  invade
          space and walls

Remembering Ben

Dogged and final he set out, as one hearing
   a distant call, one not heard by father or friend--
   a call not voiced, not in
   the insistent music of his generation.
Called by an agate? a strand of kelp, a shell? a
   glittering something on his mind's beach, jasper,
                        carnelian-- or
   just waves. Sand. Spray. Even negative ions--
Something that happens when threes meet: wind, rock, sea.

Life is full length. Leaning on air, leaving footprints,
   friends, and a trail of bright stones, he traveled
   into a melting horizon: the edge of dream a
   lodestone to his north. Were they enough, the
   mothering years and the child, breaking-away years--
   two or three backpack years, all totaling maybe nineteen?

Brief, we say, forgetting complete is just
beginning, middle, and end. Life is full length.

Ink-Spot Cat

Night stalker
back of night color, sides of bracken
belly of twilight
pond-green query in your eyes: tell me (for I
may query too) how you did it-- that this
life bursting happens in my brown study--?
Five of them, your clean and shining sons and
playfellows. On my couch back--
clinging to my shower curtain, my
leg--
my bedspread, reaching
a right hook from under a skirted
chair; at my heel (grown cautious from [ah
dear] experience)--. This is mad multiplication,
that 2 X OUT = 5 ....

Was it some elixir in the blushing azaleas, the
                              ruddy rhododendrons--?
your dahlia dalliance in the garden path--?
These merry pranksters bear no relation
to that tiger churl out
spraying on my petunias, marking
my marigolds, caterwauling in the
calendulas-- this small caperer
smells like cookies, is a fluff in my palm, purrs
like a warm dragon, happy home, a fireside beast who
sings in my silence, syncopates the even
rhythm
of my days ...

    X five.

Dearest Sir Here I Am
...Again

"Here then, I suggest, is the tiny bridge
across which came the directions which built
our civilizations and founded the world's
religions, where gods spoke to men ...."
    --Julian Jaynes, *The Origin of Consciousness
      in the Breakdown of the Bicameral Mind*, 104.

... maybe because it's 9:25 or October
looking for a door.
The Way leads down, or up--
so say my dreams

                and down is in.
You're there somewhere, and I
have a rendezvous with

      You ...

the question is: how to?

In days of yore, before
consciousness, with its augur
      (such a bore)
with its blah blah blah outnoised
        Everything
there was a voice. --You.
      I presume.
Consciousness augured ill: back
before the dust cleared we heard your
      Will
through permanent inflexible
never-fail earphones-- there,
just behind the ear.

    --Find it?--

Now: (consciousness "ever ready to explain
          anything we happen to find
               ourselves doing")
one entreats [humbly or not, depending ...]
and message tumbles
                    jumbled
  in sleep-numbed ears
     (or Jaynes or someone is
             a fool).

Dreaming's
          a pot of message--
            a stew of sorts
         nourishing perhaps and
                    indecipherable.

Maybe old Saul had it right:
    having (1) dreamed, then (2) roll bones--.
          And (3)
               ask the Dead.

But that's the lot: no other ways
    are given (honor being
without prophet in this place)
and Endor's gone, and I am not a seer.
Blind, yes, I face the dark of answers where
i wish you Are, if anything's gone right,
    to ask You, if you have a way to say:

where Were you, Sir, when Moses' light

          went out?

Entropy Rondeau

Then let us sing. We won't stay long--
What better souvenir than song
to leave for those who follow after?
(… a song, a word, a little laughter--?)
Perhaps some child will sing along …

And let folk say and ding and dong
our world is ending. They're not wrong:
it ends regardless. Are we dafter--?
        Then let us sing--

To us these moments now belong
and if we celebrate among
ourselves, I say there's no disaster
if deaths or dooms we cannot master
surprise us soon, or late, or long …
        Then let us sing.

Downhill Song

62

Salt is a simple compound, yet
it gives one's appetite a whet
and yields trace minerals, we know
(hence deer and cattle crave it so--
Cochiti traveled far to get

the stuff for tribal use). But let
earth's rivers run, and you can bet
they pick up salts each place they go--
      Salt is a simple compound.

And as the centuries abet
the water's purpose being wet,
the rivers' moving high to low,
the salts accumulate; and so
a sterile desert's all we'll get--
      Salt is a simple compound ...

even to Gomorrah

--but looking back is all that is
forward is question
blank
empty
wordless
void--
pillar of salt has more eternity
than pillar of flesh

--keatsurn, remember--

salt is.
And flesh is not so much without it.

Better, shall we say, to be Lot's wife
than Lot, awake
aware
wifeless

under orders to survive.

endurances

You must have noticed how most of it was
                    Naomi
how Naomi went in starving times
to a strange land, to Moab, with her man
and boys, and how
                    Naomi
was kind to her foreign daughters-in-law.

Naomi even took one with her, back to Judah
                once the harvest turned
                    and taught her
            how to get barley enough to get by, even
                if she was foreign
            how to get a drink of water, even if
                she was foreign
            how to keep from being raped, even if
                she was foreign, and
            how to catch a man. Even if
                she was foreign.

Naomi made her daughter-in-law a good marriage in
                a civilized country
so that the name of her son, Naomi's son
                might be perpetuated
and not cut off from among his brethren and
  from the gate of his native place.

And when the marriage of Naomi's daughter-in-law
                was blest with a son
the women called Naomi blessed: "Blessed be the
                Lord
who has not left you this day without
                next of kin"
and of the baby: "A son has been born to
                Naomi."
He was Obed the father of Jesse the father of

David

but the book was named Ruth.

Fall, or After

Conditions here outside the gate
                    offend:
Sunrise, when gibbons sing
                    brings flat despair.

Why, when mystery shrouds my canyons, over there--
      when orange light gilds rooftops--
            starlings talk the autumn miracle
            and blood springs in the veins
should humankind in metal carapace
go nose-to-ground in runnels off to serve
gods who don't at all believe in lives?

Was it for this our Adam gave his bone
            Eve her heart
            serpent his wings--?
Yearly for this the gravid Nile silts down?
for this, then, Menelaus lent his lady ...
Lesser reckonings have needed greater room.

      Sinking, sinking, sinking ...

      like drowning sailors

      ... grasping at stars ...

fine bone frames

and in the end, who is it dies--?
  Caught in the world of forms, turn and tangle,
a move, three moves, check and mate and who dies?

toddler in pink dress with pepper on her tongue--
is she the one--?
girl with peeled-willow horse, skinned knees--?
radiant young mother,
endlessly answering parent of three
     quizzical heads--?
  (reasonable parent, reasonless lover)--
       some or all of these--?
or teacher
    poet
      sketcher
        dreamer
petty pettifogging procrastinant--?

who draws the short straw?

CE NICE VERY NICE NICE NICE VERY NICE NICE NICE VERY NICE NI
ME DEVICE SO MANY PEOPLE IN THE SAME DEVICE SO MANY PEOPLE I[1]

solid as lakemist we, I, you
a kind of three-D dreamstuff
some form of amusement for All-That-Is and then

death is the thing that happens: a bubble
               pops
nothing is lost, the water is there
and the air
nothing is gone-- only a form
     and a rainbow
       … oh …
  yet
        oh.
Form is transient. Why so beloved?
  What is in the world of forms?

---

[1] Kurt Vonnegut, *Cat's Cradle*.

secret agent on planet 3

Being a spy here, set down somewhere north
of the Pishon, near Havilah, and having
obediently eaten my directives

unopened

I observe in stillness how the slanting light--
--ah, but there is little time

: it

impends, X-day, the final, ineluctable X ...

Consider, then, this X:

X is stance.

Very well, I accept that and will obey

(salute, click heels, exit smooth and smart--
those not-sees had something ... *ach, himmel*)

don my fakir's rags,
deep-dye my skin, dialects
perfected by years of practice only my
blue eyes hinting at a northern origin, I
haunt the bazaars, listen for beads
(clicking in code ... in sh'Allah)

but you do know, old chap, there's jolly little time.

Well, then ...

X is dance.

Disguised as tree, I flower to unheard music, moved
by the winds of change blowing among spheres, a
crystal chiming in the molecules, the
woodwinds winding, climaxing in a
clash of symbol cymbals
marking time ...

So then ...

                         X is tents.

Nomad. Gypsy. Who would dream I was ever a
                   northern spy, planted
                 in this garden? It was
not easy, learning to walk, rippling my roots like
        inchworms, sidewise, unseen in the night
      to stand a little further on, a little
                         closer in--

            now, though, moving on's
                   as natural as sand dunes.
                                  And it's time ...
            but then--

                         X is dense.

         --that's the problem. The air's too thick
                 for messages coded on thin song. And
              there is little time. Washed up here on

            this riverbank, I might ponder a

            bluegreen bottle

            a note folded inside it, an address
              somewhere up north, and a name I
                 almost remember ...
              some thing I had to do but
                           it is not in time ...

                  And now this X
            marking the place where
                           something is buried.
                  Oh.
         (Sketch a salute and out, easy, casual, not
                 looking back--)

      Too bad, old scout. Good show.
                  Sorry you didn't quite ...
                  but then that's rather the usual and
                       there will
                  be other assignments.

Postscript: On Muses

'Sing, Heavenly Muse ....' With these words or some variant, the ancient poet-singer begins his tale. Our imaginations shape and give body to the picture, and we are back in a Golden Age, with harp and Homer.

Yet the invocation was ancient even when Homer tuned his harpstrings, almost 3000 years ago, to celebrate in song Achilles' triumph and disaster, Odysseus' beleaguered journeyings. So matter-of-course is the blind singer's address that he doesn't bother to name the Muse in question, taking for granted we know that Mnemosyne-- Memory, Mother of Muses-- serves his hand and voice, that Calliope, lady of epic poetry, assists, and that by implication Clio, Melpomene, Euterpe, and possibly others linger half-hid in the draperies of the hall, ready to lend their aid.

How rich the poet's casual greeting, then. 'Sing, goddess,' and *epic* stands poised at the harp, while *history*, *tragedy*, and *music* wait, shadowy, in the wings. So the mood is set for the long reaches of the *Iliad*, and sweet Mother Memory and her Nine Daughters, working through the poet, body forth figures and events, letting us smell horse-sweat and sea breeze and grit our teeth on dust flying from hooves and chariot wheels.

That was then, we may think. Poets in ancient days, singers, were lucky in having beliefs that gave them inspiration, a profound sense of sacred presence, and a fitting way to evoke, through traditions shared by the audience, a context in which their creative work is set. But what aid has a poet singer now, save only the dear and useful tools Nikos Kazantzakis counted off as he shouldered them for his *Report to Greco*: 'sight, smell, taste, touch, hearing, intellect' ...? And aren't these all a writer has? And shouldn't they be enough?

Well, no. They are not quite all we have, splendid and final though they be. Nor are they, alone, enough. Not without Mnemosyne and her daughters, the inspiration and lift of our heritage, both as humans and as writers. For embodied in memory *is* inspiration; and without the past to stand on, it is not possible to be here now. We need our mental forerunners as, physically, we need the family tree, to make us; to place us in our setting with its DO-lists, calendar, and clock; to open ideas and vistas; to give us joy and courage; and to explain our presence, our *raison d'être* to the world. Possibly, even, in some dark time, these forebears-of-the-mind give us our reason for going on.

To address the Muses, or a Muse, in a specific, attentive way is to place oneself in a context of thought or feeling. *Sing, Thalia*, we may say, and our props at once appear: the smiling mask, socks and phalluses, sly wit and bawdy laughter, lila-- divine play-- and Homeric jesting, as well as, and shadowing behind, "Saturday Night Live" and "Improv Tonight." Or, *aid me, Terpsichore*-- and out come wingéd footwear, the Red Shoes and the ruby slippers, metal taps and shiny leathers, along with Greek choruses, a trailing dress, mirrored floors, glancing lights, a flung coin, ovations, time measured in bodily movement, Fred Astaire, *Swan Lake*, Mr. Bojangles, discipline and abandon, flowing scarves, castanets. And so with each of the others: no Muse, asked, is ungenerous in response to her quiet petitioner.

Clearly, the Muses did not die in ancient days with their last Greek worshipper. Perhaps enough of attention and appreciation rises to them even today-- thin trickle though it must sometimes be-- from poets, dancers, writers, singers among us, to continue to give the Muses life. But I would propose that we honor them, singly and en masse, with new energy, with more of whatever it is such deities feed on: with awareness, offerings, notice, praises, and perhaps most of all, with use. For every component of life, mental and physical, from *breath* to *shoelaces* to *coffin*, needs to be of full use, in order that it fulfill its destiny, play out its bit performance in Act II, scene iii of some life drama.

As a start in doing my part, I offer first a libation to Mnemosyne and the nine Muses, in full awareness that *spirits* and *spirit* are related. The wine should be dark to fit a classical ambience, and should come from the soil where the offerer stands. A good dark Oregon wine, then, a Pinot Noir from our foggy, complex slopes-- perhaps an Elk Cove from the Dundee Wine Cellar, or, from the Umpqua region, *Henry Estate*'s finest ...?

Then, hoping the effort may prove an acceptable offering, I propose that we renew acquaintance with the traditional roster of Muses, adding as we go certain attributes and functions, as a means of reconsidering Muse-space and thereby perhaps coming to fuller awareness of the place of inspiration in our work, in our time.

On the roster below, each Muse, with her age-old function and emblem, is shown in boldface; and everything helpful we might add is set round her in ordinary type, as a sort of verbal floral offering. If this works, the roster will make it easier for writers to find and invoke the Muse most suited to the work we have in hand, as each of us turns again to our 'sullen art,' to the sacred act of creating.

(*Note*: you may pour your libation now, if you like, not forgetting to
reserve for yourself the offerer's portion, nor neglecting to test the wine,
lest it be anything less than perfect. Pinot goes well with poetry.)

One last thing before we begin the roster proper. Let's consider for a
moment Mnemosyne, Memory, mother of the sacred Nine. She is one of
the six Titan Women; and, as Pierre Grimal puts it, she is an 'abstract
principle ... essential to the establishment of order in the world' and in
particular responsible for the 'continuity of this world,' during the eons
before Time-- before a god of time comes into being. 'Time in its
material form,' Grimal says, 'was expressed by the alternation of day and
night, and in the spiritual sense by Mnemosyne herself.'[1] Writers, by
definition, turn first to Memory-- for both form and content; for rules of
sentence and page, for feeling and connection, for patterns, names,
births, deaths, dogs, horses, seasons, weather, records, cornerstones,
parallels, and precedents-- in our search for inspiration; and it is easy to
see Mnemosyne as Timekeeper of the spirit; she holds, brimming over
and unmeasured, what *was*, before the measured moment that is Now.

Calliope excepted, we have only slight tradition that the Muses in
their turn had offspring, at least in the sense of individuals having
fathers, or names. (Where offspring are rumored, I've noted them
below.) The Muses' creative production seems related mostly to function,
the specific function of each alone as Muse. So by implication, every
person among us who creates-- music, or poetry, or stories, or lovesongs,
or anything starry or spacey, or dance or histories or hymns or plays-- is
child to the Muse of that art, orphan no more.

Here, then, in no special order, are our Nine, warm from dancing
with the Hours and Graces on the slopes of Mount Olympus, to sing at
human bidding. Bear in mind, this list is fluid, not fixed. Attributes swirl
round each Lady and settle for a particular moment, only to rise and
dissipate, making way for the needs of another occasion. Joyfully add and
delete as your work suggests; the goddess you invoke will sing for you.

Calliope ('she of the beautiful voice'), the eldest Muse, has charge of
    epic poetry. In the iconography she may be found sitting at a **desk,
    stylus** in hand, though at least one representation shows her playing
    a flute.[2] Perhaps by Apollo, as rumor has it, or by the Thracian
    king Oeager, Calliope is mother of Orpheus-- hence, Mother of
    Song; Mother of the Hero; Mother of Mistake; Mother of the
    Sacrificed Son, the Destroyed Son; Mother of Sorrows.
        To Calliope belong, then, all our stories of heroic quest and
    journey; she knows Frodo and Samwise as well as Achilles and
    Patroclos, not to mention Perçival, Enide, Tom Jones, the

Wandering Jew, Candide, Sparrow-hawk, Fire Walker Klee, and
Alice in Looking-Glass Land. Calliope's fields are heroism,
eloquence, and poetry: she holds a place of honor among her sisters.

Calliope's attitude at desk says: *I take up the pen to write it,
seriously*. Her stylus therefore is of hammered gold, and her
traveller's portfolio, fine leather, is stocked with laid paper. In
keeping with epic, which is both lofty and lively, we must add harp
and drum to her solitary flute.

Calliope's writing dress is a simple silver robe; and she keeps
ready at hand her elven traveling cloak (an elusive silver-shot green
swirl of fabric); a pair of sturdy boots; a pilgrim's staff; a crystal;
matches; a flashlight; and a coil of light and flexible rope. For
epic's dust and glory, I'd give her also, somewhere in the right
middle distance, a merry-go-round, live and in bright array ... with
music.

Clio ('the Proclaimer') is Muse of **History**; traditionally she is depicted
with **stylus & scroll**, and often with a **case of books**. Titles that
might further define Clio are these: Mother of the Past; Keeper of
Records; Akashic Librarian; and perhaps Custodian of Minutia. She
wears a lorgnette and catches her hair up in a bun; her dress is
ankle-length and dark, a book-cover blue, with touches of white at
wrists and throat. Grimal tells us Clio is mother of Hyacinthos via
Pierus, king of Macedonia, but she seems dry and distant for any
very maternal role, particularly with such a lovely lad.

Clio's work area comes equipped with a library chair and table,
a globe, a map-case, scales, smelling-salts, a telescope, lens polish,
some files smelling of mildew, a perpetual calendar, and a large
magnifying glass. She does have access to cam-corder and Mac but
prefers her quill pen and a stack of acid-free paper. Her expression
is kindly but a bit absent, for at this moment she is busy with
revisions.

Euterpe will be of special interest to modern poets, for she presides over
lyric poetry, over **music** and **flute playing**; indeed her emblem is
the **flute** or **double-flute**. That music and lyric poetry come under
one aegis reminds us: sound is a meant element, an intended quality
in poetry, and the written form merely a useful, if gallant, after-
thought for what was meant to pass from voice to ear and to be
stored in memory alone. Euterpe serves, therefore, as our reminder
of tone, of resonance; of the weight, timbre, and nuance of sounds
and the relation of word and voice; and of the mouth, where air and
flesh conspire to make meaning.

Euterpe is Piper at the Gates of Dawn. On her back she carries
Merlin's traveling harp; the songs she plays belong to the Winds of

Change. She may be seen in Harlequin suit, just disappearing over the farther hill. Or she writes, sometimes, in cold attics or in the room over a garage. Either way, she travels light, though always she keeps a functional pen and some small scrap of a notepad about her.

Thalia's field is **Comedy**; her traditional iconography includes a **wreath of ivy**. In one hand she carries the **comic mask** and in the other a **shepherd's crook**-- the latter possibly to suggest a certain bucolic rowdiness associated with Attic comedy in its beginnings. At least one source (Larousse) suggests she is mother of the Corybantes via Apollo. Her names might include Mother Courage and Moll Cutpurse along with Phoebe the shepherdess, Nicolete the minstrel-changeling, and the Rosalind of *As You Like It*. We could dub her She Who Laughs in the Teeth of It and not be far amiss. Thalia's laughter comes from the beginnings of human time; it means awareness; and it is what we can do instead of living merely as 'fed animals'[3] and then dying. Thalia includes all that is not fixed, not sterile nor rigid; yet she knows pattern: she dances the time-loved rounds of meetings, matings, misunderstandings, marriages and merriment, of falling out, philandering, festivity, folly, and feast.

Thalia means that in us which lifts, breathes, is airy, is strong, is brave enough to give birth, is light enough to set free, is accepting enough to try again, is fool enough to hope. She is laughter, *lila*, the bubbles blown by the Creative breath, the lift that makes our journey worth the taking.

Erato is Muse of **lyric & love poetry**. She is shown in iconography with a **lyre**, or occasionally some other **stringed instrument**. Her differences from Euterpe, the other lyric Muse, may be intuited if we consider *flute* and *lyre*; for the flute carries an evocative distance and solitude about it, while Erato's instrument, the lyre, accompanies voice, suggests an intimate setting. Erato is equally at home in Paris and in Nashville; her song is love, her context human, her mode mixolydian, her hair flowing, her eyes warm with understanding. Incarnate, she is Edna St. Vincent Millay; the poet-half of Dorothy Parker also supposes her long acquaintance.

Human activities most characteristically Erato's relate to creating, loving, hugging, promising, regreting, torch-carrying, suffering, taking, giving-- the old dance-- and if we see Erato as coming in rosy robes, wingéd, bright-faced, and new, if we offer her a Valentine-box, red roses, rosemary, and rue, we shall be near her essence.

To **Melpomene** belongs the entire realm of **tragedy**, the dark world, the world of shadows, of rash and ill-considered action, of the ache of vain regret. Her emblems are **tragic mask** and **sword**; she wears a **wreath of vine leaves**. Additional artifacts for Melpomene might be the black, draped gown of dignity and pain; the wig worn by judgment, the tragic player's buskins, and the coffin. Her chief colors are the red of blood and the black of mourning, but she may also come clad in the white of frozen numbness, in the deep purple of royalty and hindsight, or in the indigo of acceptance. According to Grimal, Melpomene is mother of the Sirens, whose father is the river-god, Achelous. Certainly, Sirens and tragedy seem kin.

Melpomene's attributes include the 'formal feeling' that comes 'after great pain,' the nerves sitting 'ceremonious, like tombs,' the 'stiff heart' with its questions. For though Emily Dickinson is first a lyricist sitting in Euterpe's school, she has lived in Melpomene's presence for something more than years-- as has Dylan Thomas in his "A Refusal to Mourn" and "Do Not Go Gentle." Salvatore Quasimodo, in the small and perfect "Ed è subito sera,"[4] operates in Melpomene's country; and I persist in thinking Theodore Roethke's "The Waking" also owes tone, or feel, to her.

Terpsichore presides over **dancing**. Her traditional icons include **lyre** and **plectrum**, and we've noted in passing other emblems, touching on her relation to shoes that dance forever and slippers that, traveling beyond the Emerald City, take one home to Kansas. Whatever the color, Terpsichore's footwear, her basic understanding, is wingéd. Dancers and poets alike should therefore not forget her where lightness, movement, and a little careful or fancy footwork are essential.

Terpsichore carries a dagger at her belt, short, jeweled, little more than ornament, yet serving to remind her followers that the creative spirit must sometimes stand and fight, that the dance is in some wise mock-battle, that the individual right to create *this*, *now*, in the moment, is worthy of a life-and-death struggle. Much in dance-- its taps and shine and gloss and silks, its color and flow, its stagy surroundings-- partakes of the qualities of play or display. In this respect, approaches to war are dance-like, as is war language, including phrases like 'the European theatre of war' and the 'staging' or 'orchestration' of a planned attack, not to mention war's emphasis on pennants and strutting and battle costume.

Polyhymnia is Muse of **hymns**, or **sacred song**. Larousse assigns her also 'the mimic art.'[5] Polyhymnia is usually shown without instrument or emblem; we know her by her *serious expression*, and by her **close-fitting clothes**. But the furnishings of her room should include both celestial harp and antique pump-organ, with hymn-book open on the rack. The tapestry decking her prie-dieu is richly embroidered with mantra in many languages, and her small worktable holds inkstand and quill, a stack of ready foolscap, and an hour-glass to remind us that time is the interface between human and divine and that a singer of sacred songs sings, necessarily, in time. At her feet, a pet black goat, descendant of some long-ago exiled animal, lies ruminating.

Urania has astronomy, 'star-naming,' as her sacred charge. Traditionally she is shown with **globe & stylus**. The combination of *astronomy*, *globe*, and *stylus* suggests this possibility: *what the stars write on the world*. Since astrology, 'star-knowledge,' is implicit here, I'd give her an astrolabe and a set of ephemerides, along with a tarot deck, a crystal ball, forty-nine yarrow stalks, and a set of Rune stones.

    Urania, then, is Muse of prediction and of predictive creative work, hence of speculative fiction, space stories, science fiction. Doris Lessing knows Urania well; so do Ursula LeGuin, Steven Spielberg, Robert Heinlein, and a host of others who pay her homage. But we should not omit Walt Whitman, Baudelaire, Lord Byron and others among the poets who praise the magic of the starlit dark, who say of Urania, 'she walks in Beauty.' For as Muse of the spaces that lie beyond our little earth, she is surely Queen of the Great Mystery, and 'all that's best of bright and dark / meet in her aspect and her eyes.'

Edith Hamilton remarks that the poet Hesiod once had a personal visit from the Muses, who told him something every writer will resonate to: "We know how to speak false things that seem true, but we know, when we will, to utter true things."[6] The line speaks, of course, to makers of fiction; but it addresses us as poets in particular, poetry being, as Wallace Stevens reminds us, the 'supreme fiction, madame,' and on a par with parable as carrier of truth, the essential underlying the fictive surface. When I was eleven or twelve I made some poem about poetry, much of it now mercifully forgotten. But one line I do recall, 'lying the truth is the poet's gift,' graceless though it is, still rings fairly true.

Hamilton also describes Hesiod as saying that the Muses' hearts '... are set upon song and their spirit is free from care. Happy is that person,' Hesiod goes on, 'whom the Muses love. For though one have sorrow and grief in the soul, yet when one sings as servant of the Muse, at once dark thoughts and troubles are forgotten ....'[7] A gift so great was a considerable boon to poets of ancient Greece; a poet today can scarcely need more than some mental Mt. Helicon's wooded slopes and scented herbs, with a quick dip in the Hippocrene spring (Pegasus' hoofprint, after all) when inspiration flags.

A last libation, then, to amusement, to museums, to poets and all other bemused folk, and to the sacred Nine. May the Muses live as long as forever is, whatever forever may be.

Notes

1   *Larousse World Mythology* (New York: Prometheus Press, 1965), p. 103.

2   *Encyclopedia of Classical Mythology* (Englewood Cliffs: Prentice-Hall, 1965), p. 30.

3   A Doris Lessing phrase.

4   Ognuno sta solo sul cuor della terra
trafitto da un raggio di sole:
ed è subito sera.
(In *The Selected Writings of Salvatore Quasimodo*
[Noonday, 1960], p. 134.)

Each one stands alone in the world's heart
pierced through by a ray of unlight,
and suddenly: evening.

5   *Larousse*, p. 110.

6   Hesiod, *Theogony*, from Edith Hamilton *Mythology: Timeless Tales of Gods and Heroes* (Boston: Mentor, 1942), p. 37.

7   Hamilton, p. 37 (with non-substantive minor revisions).

Index

To order additional copies of **Bone Flute**, complete the shipping information below.

Ship to (please print):
Name ____

Address ____

City, State, Zip __________________________________

________ copies of **Bone Flute** @ $11.95 each $ ________

Postage and handling $____2.00

Total amount enclosed $ ________

Make checks payable to **Ruth F. Harrison**

Address orders to   Ruth F. Harrison
                           2710 NW Bayshore Loop
                           Waldport, OR 97394-9515

To order additional copies of **Bone Flute**, complete the shipping information below.

Ship to (please print):
Name ____

Address ____

City, State, Zip __________________________________

________ copies of **Bone Flute** @ $11.95 each $ ________

Postage and handling $____2.00

Total amount enclosed $ ________

Make checks payable to **Ruth F. Harrison**

Address orders to   Ruth F. Harrison
                           2710 NW Bayshore Loop
                           Waldport, OR 97394-9515